I017763?

TOPIC

The Holy Spirit Is the Great Down-Payment for Heaven

SCRIPTURES

1. **Hebrews 2:3** — How shall we escape if we neglect so great a salvation, which at the first began to be spoken by the Lord, and was confirmed to us by those who heard Him?

2. **2 Corinthians 5:8** — We are confident, yes, well pleased rather to be absent from the body and to be present with the Lord.

3. **Revelation 4:8-11** — The four living creatures, each having six wings, were full of eyes around and within. And they do not rest day or night, saying: "Holy, holy, holy, Lord God Almighty, Who was and is and is to come!" Whenever the living creatures give glory and honor and thanks to Him who sits on the throne, who lives forever and ever, the twenty-four elders fall down before Him who sits on the throne and worship Him who lives forever and ever, and cast their crowns before the throne, saying: "You are worthy, O Lord, to receive glory and honor and power; for You created all things, and by Your will they exist and were created."

4. **2 Corinthians 5:5** — Now He who has prepared us for this very thing is God, who also has given us the Spirit as a guarantee.

5. **Philippians 3:12,13** — Not that I have already attained, or am already perfected; but I press on, that I may lay hold of that for which Christ Jesus has also laid hold of me. Brethren, I do not count myself to have apprehended; but one thing I do, forgetting those things which are behind and reaching forward to those things which are ahead.

SYNOPSIS

The four lessons in this study, *So Great a Salvation*, will focus on the following topics:

- The Holy Spirit Is the Great Down-Payment for Heaven

- Your Righteousness Is a Gift
- Now Healing Is Yours!
- Heaven Is Your Future!

The emphasis of this lesson:

When you repented of your sin and became born again, you were given a great gift — the deposit of the Holy Spirit inside you as your down-payment on your eternal home with God in Heaven. Death is not final for the Christian! Now you belong to God, and you will be with the Lord forever; this is an amazing reality that brings great comfort and peace and spurs us to share the gospel with others — so they, too, may be born again.

The Holy Spirit: Our Guarantee of Heaven

As we begin our study of the great salvation that the Lord has for us, there are two things we can remember that will help us appreciate all that He has done. First, we need to remember that salvation isn't an idea that originated with man. Hebrews 2:3 says, "How shall we escape if we neglect so great a salvation, *which at the first began to be spoken by the Lord*, and was confirmed to us by those who heard Him." Salvation started with God! We didn't choose Him first; He chose us first!

Second, we need to remember that when we repented of our sin and became born again, we received a down-payment on our salvation, which was the guarantee of Heaven. The down-payment that we received was the Holy Spirit who lives within us. In Second Corinthians 5:8, we learn that for born-again believers, to be absent from the body is to be present with the Lord. This is encouraging news for all of us who have received Jesus as our Lord and Savior. Through the great gift of our salvation, we have a guarantee of Heaven!

Heaven Is Being Present With the Lord

Whether you've had loved ones pass on or have friends who had loved ones who have died, there were most assuredly questions about Heaven. As believers, we need to know about what's going on in Heaven, and the Bible gives us insight into Heaven in the book of Revelation.

A Note From Denise Renner

The Word of God is so powerful in our lives. It is essential that every person spend time with God and study His Word in order to stay spiritually strong in these last days.

This study guide corresponds to my *TIME With Denise Renner* TV program by the same title that can be viewed at **deniserenner.org**. My desire is that through these lessons, you find the encouragement and freedom in Christ that you need. I believe the Holy Spirit is going to speak to you through the words you read in this study tool and that as you begin to use it, you will be *propelled* into the abundant life God has planned for you. I encourage you to make the effort to receive all He has for you and all He wants to do in you — it will definitely be worth it!

Whether you have walked with the Lord a long time or have just begun to follow Him, there is so much He wants to give you from His Word. He sees where you are, and He wants to meet you there.

> **Therefore do not worry about tomorrow, for tomorrow will worry about its own things. Sufficient for the day is its own trouble.**
> **— Matthew 6:34**

Your sister and friend in Jesus Christ,

Denise Renner

Denise Renner

So Great a Salvation

Published by Rick Renner Ministries
www.renner.org

ISBN 13: 978-1-6675-0592-3

eBook ISBN 13: 978-1-6675-0593-0

As you read through the scripture verses below, remember that these are not mere words simply written in a book. What Revelation describes is reality — the reality of Heaven! What we read about Heaven in Revelation is transpiring right now! In Revelation 4:8, it says, "The four living creatures, each having six wings, were full of eyes around and within. And they do not rest day or night, saying: 'Holy, holy, holy, Lord God Almighty, Who was and is and is to come!'"

As you read this verse, this amazing worship is taking place *right now* in Heaven. Whenever the living creatures give glory and honor and thanks to "Him Who sits on the throne" — the One Who lives forever and ever — then something else happens. Revelation 4:10 and 11 reveal:

> **The twenty-four elders fall down before Him who sits on the throne and worship Him who lives forever and ever, and cast their crowns before the throne, saying: "You are worthy, O Lord, to receive glory and honor and power; for You created all things, and by Your will they exist and were created."**

This passage of scripture is so exciting because when we read these verses about Heaven, we're reading about a deposit that has *already* been made in our born-again spirit. That's why we can get excited and encouraged by this passage of scripture — *one day we will be there in Heaven!* It's amazing!

And just think: If you have loved ones or friends who received Jesus as their Lord and Savior and have passed on, then they are absent from their body but are *present with the Lord.* Right now they are experiencing this great praise and adoration and glory that's being given to God!

The Holy Spirit: Our Guarantee of Great Things To Come

What else does the Bible tell us about salvation and the promise of Heaven? What does the down-payment represent to us? In Second Corinthians 5:5, we read, "Now He who has prepared us for this very thing is God, who also has given us the Spirit as a guarantee."

What has been prepared for us? A few verses back in Second Corinthians 5:1, it says that God has prepared a new body for us; a body that is made eternal for us in Heaven. When we die, we are going to take off our "earthly tent" — our earthy body — and we're going to receive an eternal one. The Bible says that we have a guarantee of this because of the down-payment that God has made in our lives when we became born again.

In the natural realm, you often put a down-payment on large purchases you plan to make — such as a house or a car. When you make that down-payment, it means you're serious about the purchase. It signals to the seller and to the bank that the house or car is now *yours*. You've staked your claim by offering the down-payment.

In the same way, God has shown that He's serious about saving us. He is showing us His purchasing power — His redeeming power! And the down-payment that He put down to stake His claim on us wasn't money or silver or gold — it was the *Holy Spirit*.

God put His very presence inside you as a down-payment for Heaven. Talk about exciting! The Holy Spirit is inside you, and His presence carries a message. He is declaring, "This person — this temple — belongs to Me." You could say that you now have a sign over yourself that says, "I don't belong to this world anymore. I don't belong to myself. I belong to God."

God Made the First Move

Did you have anything to do with making that down-payment? Were you so smart or perfect that God decided to dwell inside you? Was it because of your accomplishments? No, that didn't happen. Instead, the Bible says we are saved *not* by our works but by His grace through faith (*see* Ephesians 2:8,9).

Did you choose Him to be your Savior in your own effort? No, that didn't happen because, before our salvation, our spirit was dead; our spirit could not choose God. But the Holy Spirit came into our lives! He gave us the grace and the faith so that we could one day say, "God, I give You my life. I repent of my sin. Forgive me of my sin."

God empowered you with His grace and mercy to invite Him into your life. You didn't choose Him first — He chose you. Salvation wasn't *your* idea — it was His!

Apprehended by the Lord

In Acts 9, the Bible tells us that Saul (who would later be called the apostle Paul) was on his way to Damascus to kill Christians. Saul enjoyed seeing Christians suffer. This is the kind of man that the apostle Paul was before his conversion. He was zealous for the death of Christians because he thought their beliefs went against the Jewish faith.

But something happened as he was traveling on the road to Damascus. Acts 9:3-5 says, "…And suddenly a light shone around him from heaven. Then he fell to the ground, and heard a voice saying to him, 'Saul, Saul, why are you persecuting Me?' And he said, 'Who are you, Lord?'" The power of that light knocked Saul off his horse, and he cried out, "*Lord!*" In that very moment, he was apprehended by the power of God.

In Philippians 3, the apostle Paul used the word "apprehended" to describe the moment of his salvation. He said, "Not as though I had already attained, either were already perfect: but I follow after, if that I may apprehend that for which also I am *apprehended* of Christ Jesus" (Philippians 3:13 *KJV*). The word "apprehended" here means *to take down, to seize,* and *to conquer.* The Lord *seized* and *conquered* Saul and transformed him from someone who was killing Christians into a powerful minister for Jesus Christ.

Just like the apostle Paul, we were going through life and doing our own thing when the power of God came upon us. His power apprehended us — He *seized* us — and out of our mouth and heart came the faith and grace to call upon the Lord. At that moment we received the down-payment of the Holy Spirit. That's what happened to the apostle Paul, and that's what happened to us when we became born again.

We Belong to Him

In Philippians 3:13, Paul continued, "Brethren, I do not count myself to have *apprehended*; but one thing *I do,* forgetting those things which are behind and reaching forward to those things which are ahead." Paul wanted *to take hold of* the thing for which God had laid hold of him. And if you're born again, what Paul was describing has happened to you as well. The Lord came upon you for a purpose.

We have not yet fully apprehended or fulfilled the purposes for which God has apprehended us, but we're pressing forward. We recognize we've been apprehended; we know it was His idea to take hold of us and save us. He put in us a deposit of His very self, His very presence — the Holy Spirit — as a sign that we do not belong to this world or ourselves, but we belong to *Him.* This was His design; this was His great plan for us!

We Don't Need To Fear Death

The Holy Spirit in you is the guarantee that Heaven awaits you. And if you've lost a loved one who knew the Lord, the presence of the Holy Spirit in your loved one is the guarantee that when he or she left his or her body, your loved one was immediately present with the Lord. *As a child of God, we have access to go right into Heaven because of the down-payment — the Holy Spirit.* How comforting that is! This is part of our great salvation.

With His victory on the Cross, Jesus destroyed the power of death. Paul reminded believers that death no longer had victory over them, and the grave held no sting because death had been swallowed up in Christ's victory on the Cross (*see* 1 Corinthians 15:54,55). You don't have to fear death because it's been conquered, and you've been given the presence of the Holy Spirit inside of you as the down-payment. For the believer, death is simply a change of address. Yes, to be absent from the body is to be present with the Lord (*see* 2 Corinthians 5:8).

Present With the Lord

Could there be anything greater than to be present with our Lord and Savior? The apostle Paul knew there wasn't. While in prison, he wrote to his fellow brothers and sisters in Christ: "For to me, to live is Christ, and to die is gain. But if I live on in the flesh, this will mean fruit from my labor; yet what I shall choose I cannot tell. For I am hard-pressed between the two, having a desire to depart and be with Christ" (Philippians 1:21-23). In his heart, Paul desired to be in Heaven with Jesus. He knew the joy that awaited him in Heaven, but he also knew how important it was that he remain on earth to proclaim the Gospel and minister to the saints.

What does this verse mean? It means that you have a *great* salvation. It means that our loved ones who have passed are now present with the Lord, and what a glorious place that is! For Christians, death is not the end of life. Death is simply a new beginning — with Him. The Holy Spirit within you is the exact down-payment, and if you were to die today, you would be present with the Lord.

His Guarantee Brings Us Comfort

It's important that we understand God's promise of Heaven to the believer because when saved loved ones die, we are the ones who can offer comfort to those who are grieving. We have the Comforter inside us!

In her program, Denise shared about her experience witnessing to a Muslim. As she told him about our great salvation, the man said, "You Christians are really lucky because you know where you're going when you die. As a Muslim, I don't know yet because I don't know if I did enough good or not in my life to make it to Heaven." What a burden this man carries.

As Christians, our salvation does not depend on whether we have "done enough good or not." Our salvation depends on our trust and dependence upon the blood of Jesus and what He did for us on the Cross. We don't have to wonder what would happen if we died right now; we don't have to wonder if we would go to hell or to Heaven. We *know* that we will go to Heaven. We can be assured that Heaven will be our eternal home because we put our trust in Jesus and His finished work on the Cross. He gave us this great salvation, and His very presence in the Person of the Holy Spirit is the guarantee inside us.

When we die, we are going to be present with the Lord. This is such great news! Not only is the Holy Spirit our guarantee of Heaven, but He is the Comforter as well. And we can take great comfort in His presence every day.

STUDY QUESTIONS

Be diligent to present yourself approved to God, a worker
who does not need to be ashamed, rightly dividing the word of truth.
— 2 Timothy 2:15

1. According to the Word of God, as Christians, we do not need to fear death. How does knowing this Bible truth free you and help you to free others? (*Consider* Second Timothy 1:7; Hebrews 2:14 and 15; Psalm 23:4; Isaiah 41:10; John 14:1-3; and First Corinthians 15:55-57.)

2. Philippians 3:12 and 13 says, "Not that I have already attained, or am already perfected; but I press on, that I may lay hold of that for which Christ Jesus has also laid hold of me. Brethren, I do not count myself to have apprehended; but one thing I do, forgetting those

things which are behind and reaching forward to *those things* which are ahead." What good things from God are you pressing toward right now? According to Hebrews 12:1 and 2, what are the specific instructions the Lord gives you to run the particular race set before you?

3. Who can you turn to for comfort when you need it? (*Consider* John 14:16,26 and John 15:26 in the *King James Version.*)

PRACTICAL APPLICATION

But be doers of the word,
and not hearers only, deceiving yourselves.
— James 1:22

1. In this lesson, Denise shared that God placed the Holy Spirit within us when we were born again. In order to develop a strong sense of God's indwelling presence inside you, take time today to meditate on the rich truth found in Second Corinthians 6:16: "...You are the temple of the living God. As God has said: 'I will dwell in them, and walk among them. I will be their God, and they shall be My people.'" Intentionally live each day knowing *God* lives inside you.

2. Consider your family, friends, coworkers and neighbors. Is there anyone you know who would be blessed by knowing that God has a great salvation awaiting *them*? How can you do your part to lead them toward Jesus? Take a moment and pray for them now. Ask God for an open door to share the Gospel and a testimony of God's goodness with them.

3. How does knowing that you have the Holy Spirit within you as God's guarantee of your salvation change how you engage in life? Are you more at peace? Are you bolder to share the Gospel? Write a testimony of how the revelation of this Bible truth impacts your daily life.

TOPIC
Your Righteousness Is a Gift

SCRIPTURES

1. **Romans 3:21-26** — But now the righteousness of God apart from the law is revealed, being witnessed by the Law and the Prophets, even the righteousness of God, through faith in Jesus Christ, to all and on all who believe. For there is no difference; for all have sinned and fall short of the glory of God, being justified freely by His grace through the redemption that is in Christ Jesus, whom God set forth as a propitiation by His blood, through faith, to demonstrate His righteousness, because in His forbearance God had passed over the sins that were previously committed, to demonstrate at the present time His righteousness, that He might be just and the justifier of the one who has faith in Jesus.

2. **2 Corinthians 5:21** — For He made Him who knew no sin to be sin for us, that we might become the righteousness of God in Him.

3. **Isaiah 53:10-12** — Yet it pleased the Lord to bruise Him; He has put Him to grief. When You make His soul an offering for sin, He shall see His seed, He shall prolong His days, and the pleasure of the Lord shall prosper in His hand. He shall see the labor of His soul, and be satisfied. By His knowledge My righteous Servant shall justify many, for He shall bear their iniquities. Therefore I will divide Him a portion with the great, and He shall divide the spoil with the strong, because He poured out His soul unto death, and He was numbered with the transgressors, and He bore the sin of many, and made intercession for the transgressors.

SYNOPSIS

When you became born again, you received all the benefits of your great salvation in Jesus Christ. One of the most amazing and life-changing blessings of your salvation is that you are now righteous, justified, and free from the power of sin and death. Shame no longer has a place in your life. You can have full confidence that God loves you, accepts you, and welcomes you gladly into His presence. Respond to His love, and receive all that He has for you in Christ.

The emphasis of this lesson:

When we believed and received the work of redemption that Jesus Christ performed on the Cross, we were made righteous in Him and justified in the eyes of God the Father. The blood of Jesus made us white as snow, and in our Father's eyes, it's as if we've never sinned; we are forgiven, cleansed, and accepted by God!

In lesson one, we looked at our great salvation in Jesus Christ. It was His idea to save us. And when we became born again, we were given a guarantee of His ownership of us; the Holy Spirit was deposited inside us. We were given this perfect and precious Gift so we would have the comfort and encouragement of knowing that when we leave our earthly bodies behind, we will be present with the Lord.

In this lesson, we are looking at what our *great salvation* is all about. It's not just a "little" salvation or an "okay" salvation, but it is a *great* salvation. Hebrews 2:3 says, "How shall we escape if we neglect *so great a salvation*, which at the first began to be spoken by the Lord, and was confirmed to us by those who heard him." Our salvation is *great* — and we see that fully in His gift of righteousness.

The Gift of God's Righteousness

When you became born again, you became righteous *in Him*. For most of us, this amazing revelation takes time to sink in. We may know He loves us, but we may not realize He also *accepts* us. We are not condemned, but we are righteous — not because of what we have done, but because of what He did for us on the Cross. We are accepted because of what *Jesus* did for us. This is made evident to us in Romans 3:21-23, which says,

> **But now the righteousness of God apart from the law is revealed, being witnessed by the Law and the Prophets, even the righteousness of God, through faith in Jesus Christ, to all and on all who believe. For there is no difference; for all have sinned and fall short of the glory of God.**

This righteousness that is being revealed to us is not our idea; it's not something man envisioned or accomplished. The gift of righteousness is

God's idea, and it is received through faith in Jesus. It's not just for a select few; it belongs to *all* who believe in Jesus. We *all* need to be saved because all of humanity — every man, woman, and child — has sinned and fallen short of the glory of God.

We were in the same terrible situation that Paul explained in Romans 3; we, too, had sinned and fallen short of the glory of God. But the Good News of the Gospel is this: we have a Savior, and He came to save us! We believe on Him and have faith in Him, and He has given us the right to enter into Heaven.

Romans 3:24 goes on to say, "Being justified freely by His grace through the redemption that is in Christ Jesus." Again, everybody has fallen short of the glory of God, but because of what Jesus did on the Cross to redeem us from the power of sin, we have been *justified* in the Lord's eyes. Being justified means that as a born-again Christian, our condition in Him is *just as if we've never sinned.* This is amazing to think about — an amazing truth of who we are *in Him.*

A Picture of Judgment — and Justification

In Denise's program, she shared a story from her own life of experiencing judgment and explained the beauty and power of being justified and made righteous.

Many years ago when I was just 17 years old and still a new driver, I made a wrong turn on the road. All of a sudden, I saw flashing red lights behind me, and I thought to myself, "I'm in trouble. I've been caught."

Have you ever had that sinking feeling in your stomach of having been caught doing something you shouldn't have? Well, I was caught, and I was in trouble. When the policeman pulled me over, I immediately started crying because I was so scared! The policeman said, "I'm sorry that this happened to you, but I have to give you a ticket. You've got to go to court, appear in front of the judge, plead guilty, and pay your fine."

When I walked into that courtroom, I immediately felt guilty and judged. I had a strong sense that I had done wrong. There in front of me stood the judge, and he had the right to sentence me or to say, "You're free." I was very intimidated, but I did as I was instructed. I said I was guilty, I paid my fine, and the case was let go. It was the first time in my life that I really had a sense of being judged.

Maybe you've had a similar experience and felt the weight of judgment. You may have done something wrong, and you were caught. As a result, you felt judged. You may have wanted to escape or to defend yourself. But it was too late — you were caught and found guilty.

But imagine that on the day you stood before a judge, a kind person walked up and said, "I know you are guilty, but I will pay your fine. Put this debt on *my* record, judge. I want this person to be totally cleared. I want to pay the debt, and I want it on my account so that they are justified." That's exactly what Jesus did for the whole world. He stepped in on our behalf and paid the debt for our sin that we owed to God.

Justified by His Grace

The Bible says that God loved the whole world so much that He gave His Son, Jesus (*see* John 3:16). When Jesus was on the Cross, He took our sin, guilt, and condemnation with Him — and He did it for the whole world. He said, in essence, "I'll pay your debt. I'll make it just as if you'd never sinned." We were justified by his grace through that payment of the debt, which was made for us through Jesus Christ.

Romans 3:24 in *The Passion Translation* gives us a deeper way of thinking about what Jesus accomplished for us when He justified us through His death, burial, and resurrection. It says:

> **Yet through his powerful declaration of acquittal, God freely gives away his righteousness. His gift of love and favor now cascades over us, all because Jesus, the Anointed One, has liberated us from the guilt, punishment, and power of sin!**

Isn't that powerful? He declared you *not guilty*. He declared you *justified* — not because *you* did everything right but because of *His* perfection. *He* did everything right! And He took on all your imperfection, all your guilt, and all your shame so you could be made righteous in Him.

Jesus Became the Justifier

In Romans 3:25, we see that God is the one who initiated this work of justification; He wanted to demonstrate something through the death of Christ Jesus. What was He demonstrating? His righteousness!

> **Whom God set forth as a propitiation by His blood, through faith, to demonstrate His righteousness, because in His forbearance God had passed over the sins that were previously committed.**

In the *Old Testament*, God "passed over" the sins of His people (*see* Exodus 12:13). But in the *New Testament*, He didn't simply pass over our sins — He *became* sin for us! It was His idea to demonstrate His righteousness so that we might benefit from His amazing gift. In Romans 3:26, Paul explained the reasoning behind what God was demonstrating.

> **…To demonstrate at the present time His righteousness, that He might be just and the justifier of the one who has faith in Jesus.**

In other words, God is just. If we kill, murder, lie, cheat, take God's name in vain, commit adultery, or practice other acts of sin, God cannot overlook it. If He saw the sin and decided to let that go without judgment, then God would not be just. Someone must pay for that sin.

The good news we see in Romans 3:26 is that our sin has been paid for because *Jesus was — and is — the justifier*! Remember, just a few verses earlier in Romans 3 we read that *all* have sinned and fallen short of the glory of God. All of us in some way have offended God, and we all need this justification. Thankfully, God demonstrated His righteousness to us by sending Jesus to be the justifier! And because we've been justified, it's as if we've never sinned.

He Became Sin

The law of our land says that when we have done wrong, we must stand before a judge — just as Denise did in her teens when she made a wrong turn on the road. There is a penalty that must be paid. We must acknowledge our guilt in the judge's presence and pay the cost.

The miracle of our great salvation is found in what Jesus did for us. He said, in essence, "Father, they can't pay their debt. They can't pay this penalty. I will pay the debt for them. I will be the Justifier, and I will make it just." What a powerful gift!

In Second Corinthians 5:21, the Bible says, "For He made Him who knew no sin to be sin for us, that we might become the righteousness of God in Him." By becoming sin for us, Jesus demonstrated His righteousness for two purposes — so He could be just, and so He could become the justifier of the ones who have faith in Him. That's *us*!

He Paid the Penalty for Us

The Bible says that we esteemed Jesus "stricken, smitten by God, and afflicted" (Isaiah 53:4). Jesus entered the world as the spotless Lamb of God, but on the Cross, He became our sickness and sin — He became our lying, hate, anger, doubt, jealousy, envy, and murder.

Upon this spotless Lamb was placed all of humanity's sin and condemnation, and we could not even look upon Him (*see* Isaiah 53:3). We had to turn our faces from Him because His suffering and brokenness were such a horrible sight. Matthew 27:46 says that Jesus cried out from the Cross, "My God, My God, why have You forsaken Me?" Even God Himself could not look upon Jesus because of the sin and the death that covered Him.

But through His death, a great exchange was made! Christ exchanged His righteousness for our sin, and we became the righteousness of God in Christ Jesus. This is the great miracle of our salvation!

His Amazing Love Has Made Us Righteous

In Isaiah 53:10 and 11, we learn more about what Jesus experienced on the Cross when He became sin for us — and the result of that great sacrifice. Isaiah says,

> **Yet it pleased the Lord to bruise Him; He has put Him to grief. When You make His soul an offering for sin, He shall see His seed, He shall prolong His days, and the pleasure of the Lord shall prosper in His hand. He shall see the labor of His soul, and be satisfied....**

Why would God say that it pleased Him to bruise and crush Jesus? God was able to see through this sacrifice to the *result* of this sacrifice. God saw the torment and the horror that Jesus carried on the Cross. He saw the labor of Jesus' soul in paying for our sin — and *God was satisfied*!

In pouring out the penalty for sin upon Jesus, the need for justice was satisfied. By paying the penalty of your sin, He has opened the door of Heaven to you. Isaiah 53:11 and 12 proclaims,

> **...By His knowledge My righteous Servant shall justify many, for He shall bear their iniquities. Because He poured out His soul unto death, and He was numbered with the transgressors, and He bore the sin of many, and made intercession for the transgressors.**

Jesus knew what He was doing when He went to the Cross. He *knew* that He was bearing the sin, guilt, and condemnation that had earned us the punishment of hell. He intentionally made that choice because of His great love for us. He desired to see us freed from our sin.

God's love for us is amazing! He loves us so much that He willingly laid down His life, which paid the penalty for our sin by becoming sin for us, so that we might be forgiven, justified, and made righteous. *This is our great salvation.* This great redemption was not our idea; it was His — and it was born out of His love for us. His rescue plan saved us from eternal judgment. We have been made righteous in Christ Jesus because He gave us His righteousness!

We Are Accepted by God

Denise shared on her program that studying Romans 3 set her free from a sense of condemnation and the belief that she needed to earn her salvation. She said:

> I used to condemn myself. For example, if I was witnessing to somebody, I thought I was doing pretty good. I would tell myself, "God is pleased with me." But in my day-to-day living, I had such a sin consciousness that I believed I was unpleasing to God, and I believed that He really didn't accept me. But when I saw the truth of what I'm telling you right now, I received the amazing gift of His righteousness, and I knew that I was accepted by Him. I understood that I was *made* righteous, so that made me in right-standing with God and pleasing to Him. That truth is still amazing to me. I believe and I receive that God — the One who made the universe — came and died for me.

Ephesians 1:6 declares, "To the praise of His grace, by which He made us accepted in the Beloved." If you are born again, the Spirit of God lives in you, and you are accepted by Him. You are *accepted!* The great God of the universe — the One who made all things — came and died for you. When God looks at your born-again spirit, He sees His righteousness — He sees Jesus in you! He sees His Holy Spirit within you. And you are accepted by Him because of what His precious Son has done for you.

We Must Respond to His Love

How can we respond to such great love? We respond to His love by loving Him back, surrendering to Him, and loving others — even those who are hard to love. With His grace and mercy, God gives us the power to love them. This love He has given us compels us to be more giving and forgiving, and less judgmental and selfish.

Remember, God *wanted* you! He *chose* to redeem you. And He desires that you would trust in the blood of His Son, Jesus. It is for your salvation that He freely gave you the amazing gift of righteousness. Receive His righteousness — not because of what *you* have done but what He, in His great love, has done for you. Receive His wonderful gift of righteousness, and know that you now stand holy and blameless before Him, and love and accepted by Him!

STUDY QUESTIONS

Be diligent to present yourself approved to God, a worker
who does not need to be ashamed, rightly dividing the word of truth.
— 2 Timothy 2:15

1. According to Romans 5:17, what is righteousness? Read Philippians 3:9 and 10; Ephesians 6:14; Ephesians 1:14; and Romans 5:1. What do these scriptures tell you about righteousness?
2. Romans 5:1 says, "Therefore, having been justified by faith, we have peace with God through our Lord Jesus Christ." What does justification by faith do for our relationship with God?
3. Read Romans 10:1-10. What do these verses emphasize about our righteousness? What do these verses emphasize about our salvation?

PRACTICAL APPLICATION

But be doers of the word,
and not hearers only, deceiving yourselves.
— James 1:22

1. In the program, Denise highlighted Romans 3:21-26 and Second Corinthians 5:21. Take time to read these scripture verses several times and in various translations, then journal what it means to you to be the righteousness of God in Christ.

2. Because your sins have been forgiven, you have an amazing privilege! Ephesians 3:12 says, "In whom [Jesus] we have boldness and access with confidence through faith in Him." Hebrews 4:16 says, "Let us therefore come boldly to the throne of grace, that we may obtain mercy and find grace to help in time of need." Praise God, you have *access* to "the throne of grace." You can come boldly before Him to find help in your time of need. Take a few minutes to boldly enter His presence and share your needs with Him. He will hear you, and He will answer you!

LESSON 3

TOPIC

Now Healing Is Yours!

SCRIPTURES

1. **2 Corinthians 5:21** — For He made Him who knew no sin to be sin for us, that we might become the righteousness of God in Him.

2. **Matthew 27:26** — Then he released Barabbas to them; and when he had scourged Jesus, he delivered Him to be crucified.

3. **1 Peter 2:24** — Who Himself bore our sins in His own body on the tree, that we, having died to sins, might live for righteousness — by whose stripes you were healed.

4. **Isaiah 53:4-6** — Surely He has borne our griefs and carried our sorrows; yet we esteemed Him stricken, smitten by God, and afflicted. But He was wounded for our transgressions, He was bruised for our iniquities; the chastisement for our peace was upon Him, and by

His stripes, we are healed. All we like sheep have gone astray; we have turned, every one, to his own way; and the Lord has laid on Him the iniquity of us all.

SYNOPSIS

God has done so much for us as part of our great salvation. He hasn't left one stone unturned in bringing about everything that sets us free from all that once held us bound. In addition to forgiving our sin, taking our shame, and giving us His righteousness, He also took our sickness and disease. Through His physical suffering when He was beaten, whipped, scourged, and flogged, He carried all our physical ailments to the Cross. Through faith in His great healing power and His great salvation, we can believe — and be healed!

The emphasis of this lesson:

God loves us so much that He doesn't want us to suffer any pain, sickness, torment, or disease. He put everything that could ever afflict or grieve us or take away our peace and placed them upon Jesus, so that in Him — through our great salvation — we can be healed of it all!

Chosen By God

In these lessons, we've been learning about our great salvation and the powerful realization that *God chose us*. He arranged whatever He had to arrange in our life so that we would hear the Gospel and turn to Him. It was *His* idea — His plan of rescue for us from eternal damnation.

God loves us so much that He came up with the idea to save us. He saw our condition; we were sinners. We had missed the glory of God and fallen short. Yet He sent Jesus and He put all our sinfulness upon Jesus so that we could have a relationship with our Heavenly Father.

We have also been blessed by God to have received a deposit on the inside — a guarantee or down-payment — that when we die, we may boldly enter the gates of Heaven. And that down-payment for our salvation is the Holy Spirit who came into our lives when we believed on Jesus and asked Him to be our Lord and Savior. His presence in us is a sign that we no longer belong to this world; we now belong to Him.

Finally, we've talked about the gift of righteousness. Second Corinthians 5:21 says that Jesus became sin who knew no sin, so that you and I might become the righteousness of God in Him. But that's not all we have received in our salvation. There's even more for us to enjoy through God's goodness — and that is healing!

Healing Belongs to Us

In her program, Denise shared testimonies of God's healing power in action to encourage you and give you hope. His gift of salvation includes healing, and God is healing people and changing their lives! A woman wrote to Denise and shared the following testimony:

At the end of June, I had COVID. There was pain in my body. One night, I could not sleep at all, so the next night I took a painkiller. On Sunday, I was watching a service online and I heard Pastor Denise say, "Stand up, and raise your hands." So I stood up and raised my hands, and I began to pray with her. The pain disappeared, and it didn't come back. Glory to God! Thank You, Jesus.

That's the power of agreement and the power of the Holy Spirit in action. When we believe God, we receive what it is we believe! This woman believed God would heal her pain, and He did! Denise then shared another powerful healing testimony:

I had a bad allergic reaction to a chemical. For three days, the doctor tried to treat me with the help of shots, but nothing changed, and they did not know what else they could do for me. I could not sleep normally, and my kidneys began to shut down.

On the third day of this illness, I suddenly remembered Pastor Denise's program. The Holy Spirit reminded me of the leper who said to Jesus, "I know You can heal me, but I don't know if You want to. Jesus, if You want to heal me, do it." [See Matthew 8:2,3.]

I made the decision to pray and command the spots on my skin to go away. I told the spots, "Leave my body right now. The blood of Jesus is on me. I prohibit you to appear. My Lord, I want to sleep. Jesus, I know if You want to heal me, You can heal me." I went to bed and slept for seven hours. In the morning, I saw that all the spots on my body had disappeared, and my kidneys were working!

This woman was completely healed! She trusted in God and believed the blood of Jesus was powerful enough to overcome her sickness. And through her faith in His Word, she reached out and took hold of her healing.

Part of our great salvation is healing, and this doesn't mean healing from sickness and disease when we get to Heaven. The Bible says there won't be any sickness in Heaven (*see* Revelation 21:4). No, God has given us healing while we're still here on earth. The physical healing of our bodies is a gift to us through our great salvation.

'In That Scourge Was Our Healing'

Describing how Jesus was treated after He was arrested in the Garden of Gethsemane, Matthew 27:26 says, "Then he [Pontius Pilate] released Barabbas to them; and when he had scourged Jesus, he delivered Him to be crucified." The Bible tells us about the scourge that Jesus received before He went to the Cross. We sometimes call it "stripes" or "bruises" or "wounds" that cut into His flesh. But it is in those wounds and stripes He took all over His body that we received our healing.

In Matthew 27:26, the mention of the scourge is short — just two words. This verse states that he (Pilate) "scourged Jesus." Yet when we consider its meaning, we can see the magnitude of those two small words. In this scourge was the healing for the woman who had COVID. In this scourge was the healing for the woman whose kidneys were failing and had spots on her body from a chemical reaction.

In the program, Denise shared about the healing she received many years ago. Let this testimony encourage you! It will build your faith in the healing power of God that is available to you in your great salvation.

> Many years ago, I believed on Jesus to heal a disease that I had on my face for 13 years. In that scourge was my healing! What happened to me? I believed God's Word that I was healed by His stripes. Two months went by, but one night I went to bed with that disease just like I had for 13 years, and the next morning, I woke up and I had received a complete miracle! My forehead, my

cheeks, and my neck were clear, and the disease was completely gone.

This healing happened because of the scourge that Jesus suffered for us. Jesus didn't take on that suffering, wounding, and pain in vain. He received the scourge so that we would believe on what He did for us and receive our healing.

The Horror of the Scourge

Why would Jesus endure such horrible treatment? He did it because He didn't want you to suffer or be in torment. Rick Renner's book, *Paid in Full*, tells us what happened to Jesus when He took on the suffering that brought us healing:

> This was considered to be one of the most feared and deadly weapons of the Roman world. It was so ghastly that the mere threat of scourging could calm a crowd or bend the will of the strongest rebel. Even the most hardened criminal recoiled from the prospect of being submitted to the vicious beating of a Roman scourge.
>
> Most often, two torturers were utilized to carry out this punishment, simultaneously lashing the victim from both sides. As these dual whips struck the victim, the leather straps with their sharp, jagged objects descended and extended over his entire back. Each piece of metal, wire, bone, or glass cut deeply through the victim's skin and into his flesh, shredding his muscles and sinews.
>
> Every time the whip pounded across the victim, those straps of leather curled tortuously around his torso, biting painfully and deeply into the skin of his abdomen and upper chest. As each stroke lacerated the sufferer, he tried to thrash about but was unable to move because his wrists were held so firmly to the metal ring above his head. Helpless to escape the whip, he would scream for mercy that this anguish might come to an end.[1]

Isaiah 53:5 says, "But He was wounded for our transgressions, He was bruised for our iniquities; the chastisement for our peace was upon Him, and by His stripes we are healed." Notice that this verse in Isaiah says, "By His stripes we *are* healed." But in First Peter 2:24, it says we *were* healed. The verse reads, "Who Himself bore our sins in His own body on the tree, that we, having died to sins, might live for righteousness — by whose stripes you *were* healed." Our healing was finished, just as our salvation was finished.

He Does Not Want Us To Suffer

Let's look again at Rick's book, *Paid in Full*. This reveals to us what Jesus endured for us as He obtained our healing. It says:

> In First Peter 2:24, the apostle Peter quoted Isaiah 53:5. He told his readers, "…By whose stripes ye were healed." The word "stripes" used in this verse is *molopsi*, which describes a full-body bruise. It refers to a terrible lashing that draws blood and that produces discoloration and swelling of the entire body.[2]

Peter wrote about this experience in First Peter 2, but Peter *saw* this in person. He was there when it happened. We weren't there; we didn't see this happen to Jesus in person. But we can read about the scourge Jesus' received in the Scriptures, and it's our opportunity and great privilege to believe the Word of God.

This revelation of what Jesus suffered is not written in the Bible to make you feel guilty. It is written — and He endured it — so you could be free of pain. He did it so you could be free of sickness and disease in your body and mind. He does not want you to suffer.

Denise shared in her program about the power of realizing Jesus has already paid for your healing!

> Before Jesus healed me of the disease I'd had for 13 years, I didn't know that He took my disease on the Cross. I didn't know that He was tortured like that — not just for my sin, but for my sickness and disease too. But when that realization came into my heart that His suffering was for the very disease that was on my face, I believed it! That realization came upon my face, and I was completely healed.

Jesus Bore Your Sicknesses Already

In Isaiah 53:4, the Bible begins to describe what Jesus carried for us when He went to the Cross. It says, "Surely He has borne our *griefs* and carried our sorrows…." The word "griefs" here means *sicknesses*. If you are sick right now, or if there is some kind of sickness trying to overcome you, know that the Bible says that Jesus *took your sicknesses to the Cross.*

In the program, Denise shared a testimony of how God healed her while she was pregnant with their first son; constant nausea made it hard to even drink water. Meditating on Isaiah 53:4 and understanding what it meant to her, she decided that since Jesus had already taken her sickness, she no longer had to carry it. Standing on the Word of God in faith, she received her healing and never had another symptom of sickness during her pregnancy after that day.

Isaiah 53:4 goes on to say, "Yet we esteemed Him stricken, smitten by God, and afflicted." What was He afflicted with? He was stricken by our sicknesses! He was afflicted by our diseases! He was afflicted with every disease that might come upon us. Every sickness and disease came on Him first, and He carried them to the Cross.

'By His Stripes We Are Healed'

Any sickness that might try to afflict us, Jesus has already carried for us. Isaiah 53:5 continues, "But He was wounded for our transgressions, He was bruised for our iniquities; the chastisement for our peace was upon Him, and by His stripes we are healed."

Notice what this verse says. Anything and everything that would try to steal your peace has already come upon Jesus. That's why you can come to Him and say, "Lord, I need Your peace. Help me." And when you pray that simple but powerful prayer, His peace can come to you because He already took upon Himself everything that would steal your peace. Through those wounds and cuts in His skin (that went clear to His muscles and sinews), He paid for your healing. You are *already* healed in Him!

Isaiah 53:6 explains, "All we like sheep have gone astray; we have turned, every one, to his own way; and the Lord has laid on Him the iniquity of us all." It was the Roman soldiers who literally laid those lashes from the whip onto Jesus, but it was God the Father who put your sickness on Jesus. That is something to be thankful for! He took sickness on Himself. His body was bruised and wounded so He could carry any disease that might try to afflict you.

Believe Him Right Now for Healing

Denise shared that she had many operations and treatments attempting to remove the scars from her face, but with every blemish came another scar. But Jesus healed the sickness from her face, and the scars stopped. He took that ugly, awful sickness on Himself, and it hung on the Cross with Him.

Just like Denise received healing for the sickness that had afflicted her, you, too, can believe right now and receive His healing — for *you*! He took your sickness and disease too. Believe it because it's the truth! He took it for you, so you might be made well. God's power is working right now — even as you read this.

So if you've been worrying about sickness or bad news from the doctor, receive the power of God right now, and believe that He took every sickness and disease to the Cross. "He was wounded for our transgressions, He was bruised for our iniquities; the chastisement for our peace was upon Him, and by His stripes we are healed" (Isaiah 53:5). You are healed right now — just receive it!

Remember God didn't want you to suffer with *any* disease. That's why He put it on Jesus — for *your* sake. Don't take that sickness — don't receive it. Give it to Jesus. He took it for you, and healing is for *you* — today!

STUDY QUESTIONS

Be diligent to present yourself approved to God, a worker who does not need to be ashamed, rightly dividing the word of truth.
— 2 Timothy 2:15

1. The Bible makes it clear that healing in our physical body is part of the great salvation Jesus has obtained for us. Read several healing scriptures in several Bible versions this week and consider what they show you about God's desire to heal you.

    • "The Lord will help them when they are sick and will restore them to health" (Psalm 41:3 *GNT*).

    • "Lord my God, I called to You for help, and You healed me" (Psalm 30:2 *NIV*).

    • "The Spirit of the Lord God is upon me, because the Lord has anointed me to bring good news to the poor; he has sent me to bind up the brokenhearted, to proclaim liberty to the captives, and the opening of the prison to those who are bound" (Isaiah 61:1 *ESV*).

2. Psalm 103:3 says, "Who forgives all your iniquities, Who heals all your diseases." Why would God include healing together with the forgiveness of sin? What does that reveal about His heart toward humanity?

3. Proverbs 4:22 says that God's words are "life to those who find them, and health to all their flesh." Just as people take medicine daily, apply the Word of God regarding healing — daily — to your life. Make a plan to add healing scriptures to your times of prayer and meditation on His Word every day.

PRACTICAL APPLICATION

But be doers of the word,
and not hearers only, deceiving yourselves.
—James 1:22

1. How has reading the healing testimonies included in this lesson encouraged your faith today? The good news is that "there is no partiality with God" (Romans 2:11). And "Jesus Christ is the same yesterday, today, and forever" (Hebrews 13:8). Read the testimonies again with the truths of Romans 2:11 and Hebrews 13:8 in mind and perceive faith for healing arise in your heart!

2. Do you need healing in your body today? Read Isaiah 53:4-6 and First Peter 2:24 in several different translations of the Bible, then read the portion of this lesson on "the scourge" and allow it to infuse you with faith for healing. Glory to God, you can reach out right now as you read this and take hold of the healing power of God for yourself. Praise Him for your healing — you *are* healed.

---

[1] Rick Renner, *Paid in Full: An In-Depth Look at the Defining Moments of Christ's Passion* (Tulsa, OK: Teach All Nations, 2008), p. 171.

[2] *Paid in Full*, p. 173.

TOPIC

Heaven Is Your Future!

SCRIPTURES

1. **John 3:16-18** — For God so loved the world that He gave His only begotten Son, that whoever believes in Him should not perish but have everlasting life. For God did not send His Son into the world to condemn the world, but that the world through Him might be saved. He who believes in Him is not condemned; but he who does not believe is condemned already, because he has not believed in the name of the only begotten Son of God.

2. **1 Corinthians 15:53-57** — For this corruptible must put on incorruption, and this mortal must put on immortality. So when this corruptible has put on incorruption, and this mortal has put on immortality, then shall be brought to pass the saying that is written: "Death is swallowed up in victory." "O Death, where is your sting? O Hades, where is your victory?" The sting of death is sin, and the strength of sin is the law. But thanks be to God, who gives us the victory through our Lord Jesus Christ.

3. **Revelation 4:8-11** — The four living creatures, each having six wings, were full of eyes around and within. And they do not rest day or night, saying: "Holy, holy, holy, Lord God Almighty, Who was and is and is to come!" Whenever the living creatures give glory and honor and thanks to Him who sits on the throne, who lives forever and ever, the twenty-four elders fall down before Him who sits on the throne and worship Him who lives forever and ever, and cast their crowns before the throne, saying: "You are worthy, O Lord, to receive glory and honor and power; for You created all things, and by Your will they exist and were created."

4. **Revelation 5:9-13** — And they sang a new song, saying: "You are worthy to take the scroll, and to open its seals; for You were slain, and have redeemed us to God by Your blood out of every tribe and tongue and people and nation, and have made us kings and priests to our God; and we shall reign on the earth." Then I looked, and I heard the voice of many angels around the throne, the living creatures, and

the elders; and the number of them was ten thousand times ten thousand, and thousands of thousands, saying with a loud voice: "Worthy is the Lamb who was slain to receive power and riches and wisdom, and strength and honor and glory and blessing!" And every creature which is in heaven and on the earth and under the earth and such as are in the sea, and all that are in them, I heard saying: "Blessing and honor and glory and power be to Him who sits on the throne, and to the Lamb, forever and ever!"

5.   **Revelation 21:3,4** — And I heard a loud voice from heaven saying, "Behold, the tabernacle of God is with men, and He will dwell with them, and they shall be His people. God Himself will be with them and be their God. And God will wipe away every tear from their eyes; there shall be no more death, nor sorrow, nor crying. There shall be no more pain, for the former things have passed away."

6.   **Isaiah 41:10** — Fear not, for I am with you; be not dismayed, for I am your God. I will strengthen you, yes, I will help you, I will uphold you with My righteous right hand.

SYNOPSIS

In these last days, God desires us to be well-equipped to meet whatever the enemy may send our way. The enemy is trying to steal, kill, and destroy (*see* John 10:10), but in that same verse, Jesus said He came so we may have life — and life more abundantly. This includes salvation and healing in *this* life, and the promise of Heaven in the next. We can trust in His Word to equip us for victory at every step because we know that He saves, heals, and delivers. This gives us great peace and is the inspiration for sharing His Good News — the Gospel — with all who will hear it in these last days!

The emphasis of this lesson:

Heaven is our home once we are born again. Because we are saved by grace through faith in the Lord Jesus Christ, so many wonderful blessings await us. We can be greatly comforted by God's amazing love for us. When we go home to be with Him in Heaven, we will be ushered into His presence. There, He will wipe away our tears and give us great peace. We have nothing to fear — not even death — because Jesus has swallowed it up in His great victory!

We Have the Promise of Heaven

In Lesson 2, we saw that when we are born again, we receive His great salvation by faith. As a result of the sacrifice Jesus made for us on the Cross, God puts the Holy Spirit within us as the down-payment for our eternal life in Heaven. If you have the Holy Spirit living inside you, you have an assurance — a guarantee — that you are going to Heaven when you die.

When your body dies, your spirit will continue to live on. It's because of the Holy Spirit inside you, that at that moment of your earthly passing, you will go straight to Heaven to be with God forever. What a tremendous blessing and source of peace to know that when we believed on Jesus and trusted in Him, He took our guilt, our condemnation, and our shame, and He gave us His righteousness. None of us are perfect, but our spirit is totally perfect and righteous before God because we are born again. In Him, we are justified — it's just as if we'd never sinned. Now we can stand in God's presence because of His righteousness.

Ephesians 6:14 says that we are to put on "the breastplate of righteousness." His righteousness protects us and is a weapon against the enemy. That breastplate of righteousness covers our heart, and it covers our emotions. When the devil comes to accuse you and spew lies that you've failed, you'll never amount to anything, or you can't do what God has called you to do, you can stand up in faith and say, "No, devil! I am the righteousness of God in Christ Jesus. He accepts me as one of His own." The Bible says that the righteousness of God speaks (*see* Romans 10:6-13), and it speaks of your acceptance with the Father — because you are born again and in Him!

Heaven and Hell Are Real

We have salvation and healing in Him. We also know that our relationship with Jesus extends beyond this world and into eternity. And we all are keenly aware that people die, and when we are confronted with it, the question of what happens after death arises. It is for this reason that Jesus ultimately came: He wanted to set us free from the power of death that comes as the result of sin.

Even though many of us don't hear sermons on this subject very often, Heaven and hell haven't disappeared — they still exist. Heaven and hell are very real. The truth we must be willing to acknowledge and accept is that when people die, some of them will go to Heaven but some of them will not.

Our Eternal Destiny Is Found in Him

The difference in our eternal destiny — Heaven or hell — depends on whether we have received Jesus. Romans 10:9 says, "If you confess with your mouth the Lord Jesus and believe in your heart that God has raised Him from the dead, you will be saved." Those who put their trust in Jesus and commit their lives to Him have a right to experience Heaven. His blood washes us clean. It makes us righteous before Him. It puts the down-payment of His Holy Spirit inside us, and that down-payment is our entrance into Heaven. This is our great salvation in all its glory!

Let's look at what John 3:16-18 tells us about eternity:

> **For God so loved the world that He gave His only begotten Son, that whoever believes in Him should not perish but have everlasting life. For God did not send His Son into the world to condemn the world, but that the world through Him might be saved. He who believes in Him is not condemned; but he who does not believe is condemned already, because he has not believed in the name of the only begotten Son of God.**

This is God's Word, and we can believe it! These verses of Scripture make it clear that those who believe in Jesus are not condemned, but those who do not believe in Him are condemned already.

Death Has Been Destroyed

If you are born again, then the Holy Spirit is living inside you as a witness that you belong to Him (*see* Romans 8:16). The Bible also tells us in Romans 8:14 that those who are led by the Spirit are the sons of God. Are you being led by the Spirit? If you are born again and the Holy Spirit dwells in you, that is God's witness inside you that you are His.

When you die, you will be going to Heaven because you are born again and belong to Him. Praise God! Death for you as a Christian has been destroyed. How is this so? Jesus destroyed and stripped death of its power on the Cross. We see this in First Corinthians 15:53 and 54, which are magnificent verses that reveal Jesus' triumph:

For this corruptible must put on incorruption, and this mortal must put on immortality. So when this corruptible has put on incorruption, and this mortal has put on immortality, then shall be brought to pass the saying that is written: "Death is swallowed up in victory."

Death no longer has power over you! The horror of death has been swallowed up in Christ's victory on the Cross! Through the Lord Jesus Christ, you were given the victory over death. You do not have to fear death because Jesus defeated it! He swallowed up the power, the sting, and the horror of death, and He gave victory over it to all who believe on Him.

Think about it: How many people do you know who are afraid of dying? The Good News of the gospel is that as Christians, we don't have to be afraid to die. Jesus is victorious over death, and because we are born again, we are too. When Jesus rose from the dead, we were raised with Him. We have power over death because of Him. This is revealed further in First Corinthians 15:55-57:

"O Death, where is your sting? O Hades, where is your victory?" The sting of death is sin, and the strength of sin is the law. But thanks be to God, who gives us the victory through our Lord Jesus Christ.

Absent From the Body, Present With the Lord

The Bible says in Second Corinthians 5:8 that to be absent from the body is to be present with the Lord. The moment you take your last breath here on earth, you will be with God in Heaven. If you had a loved one who knew Jesus and has died, that person is now present with the Lord. You may have watched him take his last breath, and you may be grieving his absence from the body because you miss him so much, but if he was born again, then he is with God. Your loved one is now seeing God's glory!

When you are born again and have the down-payment of the Holy Spirit on the inside, then the millisecond you take your last breath, you will find yourself in God's presence. You'll be with Him in Heaven. It's through trusting in the death, burial, and resurrection of the Lord Jesus Christ and in His blood that we receive the guarantee of the Holy Spirit and have our entrance into Heaven.

Captivated by the Presence of the Lord

There are many quality books that have been written about Heaven, but you should certainly study what the Bible says concerning Heaven, so you can be encouraged about what awaits you as a born-again believer in Jesus Christ. For now, let's look at a few things we can learn about Heaven from the book of Revelation.

When we get to Heaven we will be captivated by the Lord! Yes, there are golden streets, and they're going to be wonderful. Yes, there are gates that are made of pearl, which will be magnificent to see. But our attention will not be on the beautiful gates, or the streets made of gold. Our attention will be on the Lord Jesus Christ and God our Father. All of Heaven will be worshiping Him. In fact, Revelation 4:8-11 tells us that this worship is happening right now!

> **The four living creatures, each having six wings, were full of eyes around and within. And they do not rest day or night, saying:**
>
> **"Holy, holy, holy, Lord God Almighty, Who was and is and is to come!"**
>
> **Whenever the living creatures give glory and honor and thanks to Him who sits on the throne, who lives forever and ever, the twenty-four elders fall down before Him who sits on the throne and worship Him who lives forever and ever, and cast their crowns before the throne, saying:**
>
> **"You are worthy, O Lord, to receive glory and honor and power; for You created all things, and by Your will they exist and were created."**

This glorious worship is already taking place, and we will simply join in once we reach Heaven! Revelation 5:9-13 reveals one of the songs that God's people are singing to Him before the throne in Heaven.

> **And they sang a new song, saying: "You are worthy to take the scroll, and to open its seals; for You were slain, and have redeemed us to God by Your blood out of every tribe and tongue and people and nation, and have made us kings and priests to our God; and we shall reign on the earth."**

Then I looked, and I heard the voice of many angels around the throne, the living creatures, and the elders; and the number of them was ten thousand times ten thousand, and thousands of thousands, saying with a loud voice:

"Worthy is the Lamb who was slain to receive power and riches and wisdom, and strength and honor and glory and blessing!"

And every creature which is in Heaven and on the earth and under the earth and such as are in the sea, and all that are in them, I heard saying:

"Blessing and honor and glory and power be to Him who sits on the throne, and to the Lamb, forever and ever!"

When we arrive in Heaven, the attention will be on Jesus — the Lamb of God who takes away the sins of the world. And we're going to be kings and priests unto our God!

God Will Wipe Away All Our Tears

What else is going on in Heaven? Revelation 21:3 says, "And I heard a loud voice from Heaven saying, 'Behold, the tabernacle of God is with men, and He will dwell with them, and they shall be His people. God Himself will be with them and be their God.'" God is with us, and we are with Him!

In Heaven, there is no separation between God and humanity! The tabernacle, or the dwelling place of God, is present with those who are in Christ. We are perfect in our spirit right now because we are born again, but we're not yet perfect in our flesh; we still have earthly bodies. But in Heaven, we'll be perfect in every aspect — and God Himself will be with us!

Revelation 21:4 continues, "And God will wipe away every tear from their eyes; there shall be no more death, nor sorrow, nor crying. There shall be no more pain, for the former things have passed away." The very God of the universe — the Creator of the heavens and earth — will wipe away every tear from your eyes.

He wipes the tears from your eyes and then He saves them. Psalm 56:8 says, "You number my wanderings; Put my tears into Your bottle; Are they not in Your book?" He keeps your tears in a bottle; He keeps track of them! Isn't that amazing? People may comfort you when you're sad, but they are *not* saving your tears. But God is!

Revelation 21:4 also lets us know that there will be no more sorrow in Heaven. Think about all the times you've cried out in anguish because your heart was broken. Think of all the times you felt heart-wrenching grief when you believed that you just couldn't take it anymore. There won't be any grief in Heaven; there will be no sorrow, no crying, and not one bit of pain.

You Are So Loved by God

What a loving God we have! He loves us with such a generous and extravagant love that can never be exhausted. He lavishly cares for us with compassion and mercy. Even the people who love you the most cannot be there for you to the depths that God is there for you. They may desire to comfort you, but they can't wipe away your every tear. They may long to help you, but they can't save you from your sin or heal your every sickness. Only God can do that!

If we could only wrap our mind around how much God loves us, we would not fear anything. We would receive His arms of love and tenderness that surround us. We would open our hearts to the One who wants to wipe away every tear, take away every pain, and heal every sorrow. That is the love that God has for you. And He's extending that love to you right now. What a glorious God you serve!

STUDY QUESTIONS

Be diligent to present yourself approved to God, a worker who does not need to be ashamed, rightly dividing the word of truth.
— 2 Timothy 2:15

1. Heaven and hell are real. Consider the story of the rich man and a beggar named Lazarus in Luke 16:19-31. What can we glean from these verses about Heaven and hell? Verse 26 tells us there is a "great gulf" between Heaven and hell. Once people die, their location in either Heaven or hell is fixed — it can't be changed once they pass from this life. How does that motivate you to share the Gospel with others now while there is still time?

2. In this lesson, Denise shared how much you are loved by God. Take time to discover even more about His amazing love for you. He loves you so much that He gave His life for you. (*See* John 3:16,17; and John 15:13.)

- **God's love for you is everlasting.** "Yes, I have loved you with an everlasting love; Therefore with lovingkindness I have drawn you" (Jeremiah 31:3).

- **Nothing can separate you from God's love.** Romans 8:31-39 speaks of God's everlasting love for you. "For I am persuaded that neither death nor life, nor angels nor principalities nor powers, nor things present nor things to come, nor height nor depth, nor any other created thing, shall be able to separate us from the love of God which is in Christ Jesus our Lord" (Romans 8:38,39).

- **God rejoices over you with singing!** "The Lord your God in your midst, The Mighty One, will save; He will rejoice over you with gladness, He will quiet you with His love, He will rejoice over you with singing" (Zephaniah 3:17).

3. Second Corinthians 5:8 says that to be absent from the body is to be present with the Lord. What else does the Bible tell us about what happens when a born-again individual dies? (*Consider* Philippians 1:21-24 and Second Timothy 4:6-8.)

PRACTICAL APPLICATION

But be doers of the word,
and not hearers only, deceiving yourselves.
— James 1:22

1. Read Second Timothy 4:6-8. Notice how Paul addresses death as a "departure." Think about those you know who have "departed." Now consider where they *arrived* after they departed from the earth and consider the captivating presence of the Lord they are now enjoying in Heaven. Take a moment to praise God — just like your loved one is praising God in Heaven.

2. Are you in a situation that seems desperate? Are you saying to yourself, "I can't take this anymore"? Whatever you may be facing, know that God is with you. Isaiah 41:10 says, "Fear not, for I am with you; be not dismayed, for I am your God. I will strengthen you, yes, I will help you, I will uphold you with My righteous right hand." Consider

what this verse means to you right now, and let it inspire your prayer and praise as you trust Him to help you.

3. God upholds you, and His great salvation surrounds you! You are righteous in Him, and He is present with you, helping you, and guiding you by His Holy Spirit. Whatever you need right now, you can reach out in faith and receive from Him; His comfort, His peace, and His presence are there for you. Receive Him into your heart, your soul, and your mind right now. Know that He has blessings, freedom, forgiveness, and healing for you.

CLAIM YOUR FREE RESOURCE!

As a way of introducing you further to the teaching ministry of Rick Renner, we would like to send you FREE of charge his teaching, "How To Receive a Miraculous Touch From God" on CD or as an MP3 download.

In His earthly ministry, Jesus commonly healed *all* who were sick of *all* their diseases. In this profound message, learn about the manifold dimensions of Christ's wisdom, goodness, power, and love toward all humanity who came to Him in faith with their needs.

☑ **YES, I want to receive Rick Renner's monthly teaching letter!**

Simply scan the QR code to claim this resource or go to: **renner.org/claim-your-free-offer**

Connect

WITH US!

www.ingramcontent.com/pod-product-compliance
Lightning Source LLC
Chambersburg PA
CBHW071653040426

42452CB00009B/1857